VILLA NEGATIVA

T0159943

Villa
Negativa

A MEMOIR IN VERSE

SHARON McCARTNEY

BIBLIOASIS
WINDSOR, ONTARIO

Copyright © Sharon McCartney, 2021

All rights reserved. No part of this publication may be reproduced or transmitted in any form or by any means, electronic or mechanical, including photocopying, recording, or any information storage and retrieval system, without permission in writing from the publisher or a licence from The Canadian Copyright Licensing Agency (Access Copyright). For an Access Copyright licence visit www.accesscopyright.ca or call toll free to 1-800-893-5777.

FIRST EDITION

Library and Archives Canada Cataloguing in Publication

Title: Villa negativa : a memoir in verse / Sharon McCartney.
Names: McCartney, Sharon, 1959- author.
Description: Poems.
Identifiers: Canadiana (print) 20200338145 | Canadiana (ebook) 2020033817X
ISBN 9781771963497 (softcover) | ISBN 9781771963503 (ebook)
Classification: LCC PS8575.C427 V55 2021 | DDC C811/.54—dc23

Edited by Zachariah Wells
Copyedited by John Sweet
Cover and text design by Gordon Robertson

Published with the generous assistance of the Canada Council for the Arts, which last year invested $153 million to bring the arts to Canadians throughout the country, and the financial support of the Government of Canada. Biblioasis also acknowledges the support of the Ontario Arts Council (OAC), an agency of the Government of Ontario, which last year funded 1,709 individual artists and 1,078 organizations in 204 communities across Ontario, for a total of $52.1 million, and the contribution of the Government of Ontario through the Ontario Book Publishing Tax Credit and Ontario Creates.

PRINTED AND BOUND IN CANADA

This book is for B.H. Boston.

CONTENTS

Pain on Waterloo Row

There are two ways
to walk home.

He lives on one street.
His beloved lives on the other.

I Am Not Who I Am

The urge to text is always there,
like the unopened Zinfandel left by the fabricator.
The easiest thing is to not touch it.

* * *

At night, in bed, I read.
Eichmann in Jerusalem.
In the Freud Archives.
Anna Karenina ad nauseam.

* * *

The fabricator and I slept side by side
for three months with nary a touch.

Then he posted a photo of himself,
posed with an arm around his fibreglass porpoise,
captioned it "a tender moment."

* * *

Me: "What's going on with you?"

The fabricator: "I don't
see this going long term.
I'm not in love."

Me: "That's okay.
You have a few things here.
I'll gather them up so you
can take them with you."

The fabricator: "You mean we're breaking up?"

      * * *

I am greedy with mornings.
I want them all to myself.

      * * *

The fabricator's addled ex,
the one who broke into my house
and confronted the two of us in bed,
said to him, "You must be gay
to like someone so butch."

I told the gym crowd that
and they all high-fived me.

      * * *

To know that we know.
Recursive consciousness.
This was the fall.

      * * *

When I said, "You're a handsome man,"
he said, "I'm really not."

* * *

You know those little sour cocktail onions?
Those, I love.

* * *

Eighteen days after we break up,
the fabricator texts. He wants
to help me insulate my attic.

"You buy the batts,
I'll blow the material in.
Two hours for ten batts."

My attic needs insulation,
but do I need two hours
of the fabricator?

* * *

When he texts, "Hope ur doing ok,"
what he means is, "I can't believe you could be okay."

* * *

The fabricator: "I hope you
know that if you ever need a friend,
I am here for you."

Me: "I would like my house key back
and my Bernd Heinrich book
that's by the microwave in your kitchen."

* * *

Gathering up the fabricator's last few effects—
slippers, dress shoes, razor, Gurdjieff book (unread)—
for him to pick up later.

That joy in shedding.

* * *

He left a note:
"I'm sad about this but I know it has to be this way."

He started it.

* * *

The best books have coffee stains on the covers.
They're the ones I take to bed with me.

* * *

I was the "ugly bitch" and he was the "limp dick bastard."
I said, "Don't engage," but he continued to text her.

* * *

Each man, each breakup, each failure
shows me what I am not.

* * *

From the husband:
warm the teapot with boiling water before you brew the tea.

From the pilot:

modern car engines don't need to "warm up,"
even in winter.

From the married man:
do not get involved with married men.

From the sculptor:
flutes can be incredibly annoying.

From the banker:
when I drink too much, I have sex with people I should not.

From the fabricator:
you don't have to flush every time.

       * * *

My son's needy ex sees Alan Watts'
The Wisdom of Insecurity on my coffee table,
says, "Wow, I must be really wise."

       * * *

He asked to borrow $500.
I emailed it immediately.
He texted, "Thanks,
you're a good friend."

He meant that's all you are.

       * * *

He told me that he had broken up with her.
I learned later how he defines "breaking up."
He pulls away and you have to figure it out.

* * *

She was distraught, in need of compassion.

Yet, I feel that she should not have entered
my home unbidden and called me names.

* * *

I never feel so well cared for as in
my remarkably handsome dentist's
chair, his kind solicitude as
he leans over me, needle in hand,
saying, "You'll feel a pinch now.
And your heart rate might rise."

* * *

I am addicted to mornings alone,
to silence and solitude.

Last night's freezing rain
solid on the sidewalk.
A squirrel's skeletal tracks.

* * *

The fabricator's ex-girlfriend's Facebook message to me:

"Hello! U might remember me from early Un sat marning
when u were in bed with My boyfriend that I have been with
for over a yr! He and I have been very close and care deeply
for each other! He even sings with my 11 yr old daughter that
just lost her dad a yr and a half ago! I have 6 kids who all love
[redacted] very much and all our friends said we were en
perfect together!! So u helped screw it all up for all of us! Not

just me!! [redacted] is v ery charming gb and loveable but very mixed up for 62!! Trying to on reinvent himself! I guess I come with too much respnsibility and not enough hm money for him!! Eventho he and I have soooooo much in common and are so much alike!! He adored me at 1st but got cold feet to get more serious, thats when he contacted u! But don't think u were the only one! I saw his emails!! There are others too and he admitted today in our very long talk that he will continue looking around and that he s not planni g on being ur boyfriend or anyones rt now! Ask him about the halifax girl he was ready 2 go s ee last month! She stopped it b4 he went cua she realized what a serious relationship he and I had and the good woman she is, didnt want to interfere and knew I had already been thru hell with losing my husband! Plus she told [redacted] she wanted someone trustworthy and faitful which he is not! I ve known him 25 yrs and I should have known better too with his track reacord of women and cheating! Evenwith his physical problem he is still looking for other women, when u would think he would be hesitant to??? I was v ser y patient and loving with him and he had agreed to see a counsellor with me just last week to see whT we cud do and y he was heaitant to commit deeper and long term with me! Then I caught u 2, eventho he denied he liked u in thatnway!! He lies and cheats!! And can look u rt in tthe eye and lie! Not a good sign! So woman to woman be aware!! He will be looking for someone else while with u! He yold me today there are many other woman he has been in touch with and interested in! Soooo...? Good luck, I am starting to feelrelieved he set me free to mind a honest man instead !!!"

* * *

Yes, she came in the unlocked back door,
past the ineffectual dog, to find the fabricator and myself
in bed upstairs, but she took her shoes off first.

She said to him, "What do you see in her?
Is it because she keeps a nice, clean house?"

I was starting to like her.

* * *

The fabricator hurt me.
Please forgive my lashing out.

* * *

Approval is a burden, how it engenders duty, obligation.
We train dogs with positive reinforcement.

But rejection—the slammed door, the shrugged shoulder,
the dial tone—sets you free.

* * *

If your boyfriend's ex
breaks into your house, call the cops.

* * *

My dating logic:
whether I like you or not,
you better like me.

* * *

I leave Nadya's birthday party early, in pain,
not because of Lisa's nosy questions about my breakup (that's
    just Lisa),
but because I answered them.

* * *

She was right about him, but
"to mind a honest man instead"
still cracks me up.

* * *

I take the refrigerator apart, wash all the parts
and put it back together again.
I can't stop opening the door now.

* * *

Work, gym, dog, reading, writing, sleep.
No room in my life for a man.

If I needed a man, there would be room.
If there was room, I would need a man.

* * *

Even in the marriage, I sought solitude.
Moved into my own room. Shut the door.

How politely the husband knocked in the evenings,
inquiring whether I wanted more wine.

I always did.

* * *

Do I need to be alone or do I want to be alone?

* * *

I do not want anyone,
but I also do not want to be seen
as someone wanted by no one.

* * *

I thought that leaving the marriage
meant finding someone else.
I was almost right.

* * *

Let the gossips gossip. Ashes, ashes.

* * *

Saturday night, winter solstice eve,
I'm in bed by eight with Edith Wharton,
a Thermos of cinnamon apple tea.

With less content in my life,
I am infinitely more content.

* * *

When our selves are entirely subjective,
the product of our interior dialogues,
we must be the object of something
in order to be real. Or of someone.

* * *

My childhood in the wild mustard
arroyos of southern California.

One coyote howled,
then the others started up.

* * *

All forms of addiction—
alcohol, gym, relationships—
are forms of self-betrayal.

So much easier to put my faith
in someone or something external.

I know what is right and what is wrong.
So act on that.

* * *

The task is to know what I want,
which is to be alone and clear-headed.

* * *

Do I share too much?
Very well then, I share too much.

* * *

Alone, alone, oh to be alone.

* * *

Is it possible to live with and love someone
for whom you have lost respect?

* * *

The best New Year's Day in decades.
Unhungover and alone.

* * *

My "I don't give a shit what people
think about me" attitude is bullshit.
I want people to think that I am
a person who does not give a shit
about what they think about me.

* * *

I trusted the husband's judgment.
The error was not his judgment.

* * *

I trusted that what he wanted was good for both of us.
I trusted that he wanted what was good for both of us.

* * *

All that worry about what others think,
that striving to appear well.

If I am at peace with myself,
the opinions of others are inconsequential.

Provided that I am not a psychopath.

* * *

From my basement office window:
milky winter willows furrowing an azure sky.

Soon, soon, the company will be shuttered.

* * *

The length of the marriage was a function
not of its quality, but of our dependence.

The first thing he said that he liked about me?
That I looked after my own car—the tires, the oil.

Why make a point of that?

* * *

Our bodies are vehicles for consciousness.
Pain, for example, that inflammation in my left
knuckle that depresses me so, merely
tells me what I am not.

* * *

Be not afraid.

* * *

Carmel said, "Yes, quitting smoking was hard,
but look at my new cleavage!"

* * *

We are only leashed to fear for as long as we try to be brave.

* * *

The purpose is not external, but internal.

* * *

Mother asked, "If you read so many
books, how can you have your own ideas?"

I ask, "If you don't write it down,
how do you know what it is?"

* * *

The mice that have carved a homestead
in the temperate cavern behind my downstairs
bathroom's pocket door are unaware that the debris
of their industry, wall lint and splinters, spills
out from under the electric baseboard heater
during the night, betraying them.

* * *

The two poets said that I must alter my poem
because it made me look like a wannabe.

Seriously. They said that.

* * *

Why do I participate?

* * *

Sunday morning, February 1, 2015.
Brutal externally, cold and stormy.
Brutal internally, cold and stormy.

* * *

Two days after we broke up, the fabricator posted
"8 Signs You're In a Relationship Worth Keeping."
I interpreted this as a dig at me, that I was not worth keeping.
Two months later, I look again. It's gone. Deleted.

* * *

To perceive something, we have to be able
to stand away from it.
This is why we cannot define consciousness.

* * *

The extent to which a person is consistently tardy
is in direct proportion to his or her self-involvement.

Said the person who is obsessively early.

* * *

I wanted to be cool (which I am not)
so I married the husband,
who was cool.
He went along with it.

When he wanted someone else,
it was not cool.

* * *

His need to be with people, anyone,
drinks with the grad students,
relationships no matter what.
Yet, for years, his back turned to me.

* * *

His relentless socializing was a function
of his discomfort with people.
But what was my fidelity to him?

* * *

When I express my annoyance with Facebook,
my son rolls his eyes. "It's all just advertising."

* * *

I do not know what I am,
but I do know what I am not.

I am not someone who knows what I am.

* * *

Aggression is fear, projection,
the feline's arched spine, attempting
to mask the pathos, the weakness
that renders us vulnerable.

The hard thing is to trust in the whole,
to go on when there appears to be
no reason to do so.

* * *

It was all my own damn fault
and alcohol doesn't even help anymore.

* * *

Minus 26 outside with the sun shining.
Ever more brutish. A blizzard anon.

* * *

The husband was transcendence.

Every bartender knew our names.

* * *

If the task is inward, how do I find
what is inside that will take me out of myself?

There is no outside of myself.

* * *

If you never exert yourself,
how do you know who you are?

If you're never alone,
how do you know who you are?

* * *

If my love for the husband died because he loved another,
what I felt for him was something else entirely.

* * *

If I had really loved the husband,
I would have wanted him to be happy,
to have his you-know-who.

* * *

The way I love my children,
wanting what is best for them
as they would define that,
not as anyone else would.

* * *

It was the 1970s in southern California.
Everyone was stoned.

I would smoke a joint in the tumbleweeds behind the house,
then lie on the white shag in front of my father's Fisher stereo
with Emerson, Lake & Palmer on headphones.

Later, I drove the green Chevy wagon up I-5 to the Carlsbad
mall.

* * *

Is there anything as predictable as regret?
Whatever you decide, it will seem wrong down the road.

Except for my decision to clear the snow from my roof.
That was smart.

* * *

My love of silence, of solitude,
is a love of death.
When it arrives, it will be as an old friend.

* * *

Silence was my family's unspoken rule.
So many names excluded from the obituaries.
Loneliness feels like home.

In a man, I look for someone
who will leave me alone.
This is harder to find than you would think.

* * *

In the dream, I was in bed with Alec Baldwin,
under a white duvet. No sex, just sharing the bed
and he was simpatico, cracking jokes,
long grey hair dusting his brow.
My deceased father, in the next room, approved.
I woke up happy and stayed that way.

* * *

In my solitude is my salvation.

* * *

In the first few weeks, the luthier tells me
over and over how wonderful I am, what
an inspiration I am. I am the love of his life.

I tell him this is too much pressure.

He responds, "I don't want you to feel pressure,
because I can't lose you."

* * *

Whatever you hang on to will be lost.
Hang on to that.

* * *

The more he tries to please me,
the more he pushes me away.

* * *

You cannot decide to love someone and you
cannot decide not to love someone.

Love is what we are, not what we do.

* * *

What has ten years of separation taught me?
I cannot unlove him.

To deny that is to deny love.

* * *

In the dream, there was a clause
hidden in an addendum to the contract.
It said I had permission to sleep.

* * *

More red wine and coffee
spilled in my bedroom in two months
with the luthier than ever before in my life.
By the luthier.

* * *

While colouring my hair, Paula says, "He's a man.
He's just afraid you're going to break up with him.
Don't worry. He'll relax."

* * *

The clause really said I had permission to love.

* * *

When the husband and I slept together that first time,
I was happy. I didn't care if it was just that once.

I told Jill that the next day at the diner in Coralville.
I loved him and that was enough. Even now.

* * *

I do not love lightly or temporally.
This is not a weakness.

* * *

I left not because I did not love him,
but because I did.

* * *

The luthier's fear of driving me away
drives me away.

His fear that he will insult me
is insulting. His condescension.

* * *

I say, "Please, just be yourself,"
but what I really mean is
"please be someone I can like better."

* * *

When he puts his beer beside my phone,
I get the jitters.
I can't afford a new phone.

* * *

I accuse the luthier of being too romantic.

Me, the one who still loves her ex.

* * *

The luthier drains me, his forced guffaw
at every joke, how he agrees
with everything I say.

No one is that funny or that right.

* * *

I turn my back to him
the way the husband turned his back to me.

He thrashes in bed, tossing,
loud exhalations, angry with me.
It touches me not.

* * *

In the dream, my employer had gone belly up
the previous week. Everyone knew but me.
I arrived to find a few people still working.
One said, "Didn't you hear?"

* * *

When the luthier delays responding to me, I fantasize
that he is finally fed up.

Then, an "I love you" email arrives.

* * *

The luthier sees the world as a place in which he is rejected.

* * *

He says, "This is who I am. I do things for people."
He builds my fence. He drives to PEI
with a trailer to help my son move back home.
They have to make two trips.
He lets the dogs out and makes the coffee.
He checks the mousetraps and the wires in the basement.
He buys the wine. And the beer.

* * *

Beware the man of whom it is said by all, "He's a nice guy."
He hides himself.

* * *

The husband was called by some "an ass" and "a loose
    cannon."
Poor dead Rick from Saskatoon said, "Someone should
    punch that guy."

The husband's only fault was that he was himself.

* * *

At the dinner party, the luthier is seated one seat away from me.
He seethes.

He carries dishes into the kitchen for our tedious host,
grimly helpful, as always.

* * *

Fewer phone calls, no weeknight sleepovers.
The luthier knows. He's not dumb.

His golden retriever is at peace,
but he is not.

I strain to relax.

The luthier drapes himself over me to sleep.
I shrug him off.

Then the arguing in bed.

"You're the most undemanding person I have ever been with.
I have to think up things to do for you."

I have no idea what he wants.

I fear it's a failure of forgiveness on my part,
my mother's stubbornness. At first, her new tenant
was the finest ever, a prince. Then, he was a drug dealer,
a crook. No middle ground.

I cannot forgive the luthier his discomfort, his diffidence,
the way he twists, elfin, on the sidewalk
to get out of my way.

The first breakup:

his parting shot to me, before slamming the car door and
     driving away:

"I'm just a loser and I'll always be one!"

I am alone, puzzled, in the 2 a.m. driveway.
How was that meant to hurt me?

*   *   *

O luthier, I did love you, you intense, fraught little man.
The most unsettled intestinal tract I've ever witnessed,
always churning. We both pretended not to hear.

*   *   *

He said, "I wish we could just relax and talk."
I said, "We don't talk. You just agree with me."

He neither agreed nor disagreed.

*   *   *

How he wept, hanging on to me.
I stroked and stroked his back.

He pleaded, "Please, don't do this.
I can be better."

Because begging always works.

*   *   *

If I pedalled, he pedalled.
If I coasted, he coasted.

If I ordered a burger, he ordered a burger.

Once, at the Rogue, I made him order first.

That made him angry.

* * *

He had a rough morning building the screen door,
couldn't find either of his staple guns,
so he went out and bought a new one.

He said, "I hate losing things."

* * *

On *Frasier*, Roz complains about the desperate date
who laughs too hard at her jokes.

* * *

Love is not expectation,
not resentment, not the luthier
becoming "quiet" because I failed
to scoot over on the sofa.

* * *

The luthier stroked his dog and said,
"You're the best dog."

Then the luthier looked straight at me and said,
"I've been trying to give him extra cuddles.
He needs extra cuddles."

I pretended not to know.

* * *

I thought that was what I wanted:
someone who wanted to be with me,
who wanted me above all others.

I do not want that.

* * *

I feel buoyant, peaceful after the luthier,
his myopic focus on me, lifted.

The headaches vanish, the jaw unclenches.

Then he phones. Says he has been
soul searching. I agree to a beer.

* * *

The luthier calls me "robust, sturdy."
This fills me with horror,
the old dread.

* * *

The drink with the luthier goes okay.
A rapprochement.

Afterward, we walk the dogs, holding hands.
And then, I go home to bed alone.

* * *

In the dream, I am in a department store,
taking the elevator up to the luxury floor,
the high-end goods that I cannot afford.

I step on partway, hesitating,
and the door will not close.

Finally, I step all the way in.
The elevator careens sideways and then flips,
upside down, and freezes, stuck.

I hear voices outside.
People are being rescued.
The rescuers are having trouble finding me.

* * *

He says he loves me more than he has loved anyone
ever in his life. He says he will be different.

* * *

The luthier frowns at Café 540's craft beer chalkboard,
saying, "They don't have your favourite stout."
To him, this means we must leave.

He refuses to walk through a doorway
before me, always hanging back, waving me
forward with a flourish. O lord.

* * *

Perhaps his kindness is merely kindness.
Not weakness. Not narcissism. Not self-sacrifice.
What, then, is my irritation?

* * *

The urge to get out is always an urge toward
frustration. I was an anorexic. I eat privation.

* * *

Adam Phillips says, "Look at who frustrates you.
That's who matters to you."

* * *

When I don't want to shower with him after running,
he sulks.

* * *

The second (final) breakup:

an argument over our pork tenderloin.
He stomps out of the house, snarling,
"The harder I try, the worse it gets."

I grab the dog and skedaddle.

* * *

What do they mean when they say,
"This is who I am"?

* * *

In an email, he says, "I know that I should say
'thank you and goodbye' but I can't."

Two days later, he leaves a CD in my mailbox,
Bach's *Six Suites for Solo Cello*,
with a note that says merely "goodbye."

* * *

All that effort to make me happy,
building the fence, installing the track lighting.
And the gifts: a porcelain bowl, a plush bathrobe, Irish linen.

What else was he trying to make me?

      *   *   *

His frustration mattered more to him than his desire.
He had me. He pleased me. I told him that.

      *   *   *

The luthier did not want me.
The luthier wanted wholeness.

      *   *   *

Halloween morning 2015, I wake up
to a Russian plane crash in Sinai,
224 dead. A Romanian nightclub fire,
29 dead, and the hackers have sent
more spam in my name.

      *   *   *

Let the others accelerate, gunning
their engines toward the stop sign.

      *   *   *

Just to dwell, peacefully, abiding with myself,
the way I sat beside Mother while she died.
The manna of that.

      *   *   *

Twelve months' notice at work,
the company folding.
We are too many.

*   *   *

The luthier and I attempt to be friends, dining weekly
at the Rogue, but the luthier holds his knife
with a self-conscious flourish, incising his chicken Caesar.
This I cannot bear.

*   *   *

The husband so grim on those rare occasions
when we converse.
Gets angry when I ask, "Are you okay?"
What is he afraid of? I fear for him.

*   *   *

In black November's bare-branched gloom,
two crimson cardinals bicker,
startling my solitude with their dispute.

*   *   *

I tried to cajole the dog, to comfort,
but all I did was make him anxious.

If you worry about him, says the dog trainer,
he thinks that there is something to worry about.

Just shut the door and walk away.

*   *   *

What I love most about Facebook:
the people who go on Facebook
to tell everyone they're leaving Facebook.

* * *

In all the dreardom of pending unemployment,
one thought heartens me:

there is no man in my life.

* * *

Whatever you say you are,
that is what you are not.

The luthier's, "This is who I am.
I am quiet!"

* * *

If I cannot define who or what I am, there is no
reason to regret who or what I might have been.

* * *

My preteen self, shoop-shooping alone in my
purple bedroom to *David Live*.

* * *

When I say, "This is who I am,"
I am not who I say I am.

I am the entity that says,
"This is who I am."

34

* * *

I catch myself, one December morning,
before starting the new government job
with its rigid, onerous schedule,
thinking, "I can't work that way,
that's just who I am."

* * *

"This is who I am" is an excuse,
a refusal to accept the responsibility
to change, to grow. Shrugging that off.

The surly pigeon-feeding neighbour juts her chin
at me in the driveway: "This is who I am!"

The luthier sulks.

* * *

When I say, "This is who I am,"
I am a stranger to myself.

* * *

I am the aged Jack Russell sleep-twitching on the afghan,
the raspy grader clearing last night's meagre snow
from the gutters, the man who exits the rooming house
every morning before six to shuffle downtown.

All of these and the old house crackling
into itself and my children, adults
now, as they straddle the foundering cob of this world.

* * *

I do not want the luthier.
I do not want the fabricator.
I do not want the husband, though I love him, or anyone else.
If I want anything, it is only to want.

* * *

The luthier said, "I can't lose you."
In this way, he gave his life meaning.

* * *

I said to the husband, "You don't need me."
To me, this meant that he did not love me.

Whether or not he loved me,
the mistake was mine.

* * *

Josipovici says, "The sin of despair
is the mirror image of the sin of pride."

* * *

Freud says the unconscious knows no negation.
The patient's "it's not my mother"
means it is his mother.

"I hope I did not alarm you," the luthier said
after his ultra-dramatic email about the fire.

* * *

I eschewed organized religion because the religious
experience mattered to me.

I eschewed the husband for the same reason.

* * *

I used the married man to get back at the husband,
to show him that I was desired.

Benjamin Franklin said, "Whatever is begun in anger, ends in
shame."

* * *

Let the grey hair grow in.
Why would I want to appear younger than I am?

* * *

After months of silence, I email the luthier
to say happy birthday. I do not expect a response.
I just hope he has a happy birthday.

My son says, "Leave him alone."

* * *

The luthier's odd combo of egotism and abjection:
he was convinced that I would never adore
him the way he felt he deserved to be adored.

* * *

Freezing rain on Good Friday makes for an especially
ravishing morning. Even the ravens are mum.

* * *

There is no other. Whatever pain I cause,
I cause to myself.

* * *

I will never be "over" the husband.
Why don't you get over your expectation
that I will get over the husband?

* * *

Loud pipes on the motorcycle, loud music in the car,
loud voices on the sidewalk. Why is volume always required?

* * *

I fill the emptiness by thinking about how people
fill the emptiness. I don't know what else to do.

* * *

The poet treated my non-poet friend like dirt until
she realized that my non-poet friend dated the important
poet.
Then the poet said to me, "I hope I didn't offend her."

* * *

The dog's flea medication includes a sticker to remind me of
his next treatment.
My Communist son sees the calendar.
"Hey, look! The revolution's this month."

* * *

Be the valley. Be the canyon.

Be the eroded gully where the child plays.
Three house cats quietly observing.

* * *

So many years ago, during a reading
at the JBI in Victoria, an old guy sitting
at the bar yelled out, "Ah get over it!"

* * *

Forgive the ego. It knows no better.

* * *

At forty-four, Levi knew he was dying.
The brain tumour was inoperable.
He and Dymphny arrived with their young boys
for a last visit, a goodbye while he was able.

The husband, trying to make it like old times,
offered Levi a beer, but Levi declined.
Alcohol was nothing to him now.

* * *

Neither inside nor outside.
Neither past nor future.

* * *

I bristle at what appears to me the falsity
of others, the fake laughs, the posturing,
how the woman at work stomps importantly
in her ungainly heels.

The fear that their positioning belies, the need.

* * *

"You spot it, you got it," says Holder to Linden.

* * *

A grey curl graces my keyboard.

* * *

The Taoists say, Whatever you resist, you become.
If I resist nothing, will I become nothing?

* * *

My father, days from death,
a frailty in his voice that I had never heard before,
said, "I'm not afraid to die.
I'm just worried that I'm going to miss everyone."

Every morning, I check the weather in the cities
where my sons live.

* * *

Beware, whatever you wish upon others
will be visited upon you, sure enough, with time.

* * *

No edges, no boundaries.
The sun is always over the yardarm.

* * *

No yardarm.

* * *

I am not who I am.

* * *

Heard from the open door of the Brunswick Street Baptist
    Church
on a hot August morning: "... sexual immorality, impurity,
    lies and evil desires!"

Heard from the open door of St. Anne's Chapel two blocks
    away
on the same morning: a Bach chorale.

* * *

The geese in the air are not heading home.
They are home.

Agonal and Preterminal

Susan appears agonal and preterminal.

From a neurological consult report dated September 18, 1979, eleven days before she dies.

Agonal.
Of or related to great pain.
As in the agony of death.

She was in pain.
I never thought about her being in pain.

Her hospital records indicate her primary problem began with
   seizures in 1961.

A malignant glioma in the left temporal area, excised
surgically in January 1961 at the Mayo Clinic.
Rochester, Minnesota. Then, radiation. She is eleven years old,
my big sister by ten years. I am the baby.

Mother calls it "cobalt treatment." Old black-and-white
zigzag-edged photos from Rochester, before the treatment,

show Susie, grinning maniacally from behind a monstrous
snowbank and lobbing snowballs toward the camera.

We live in an ivy-green bungalow in a new subdivision
in Sunny San Diego. Three white birchbark willows
congregate in a curved brick bed by the driveway.
I pedal my purple Sting-Ray with its glittery banana seat
and tassels to May Scott Marcy Elementary School.
Except for Susie, we are like everyone else.

She has grand mal seizures. We call them spells.
When she has a spell, we say, "Mother, Susie!"
Mother comes and strokes Susie's brow
until the seizure passes. She kneels
and cradles Susie's head in her lap.
This happens daily and everywhere.

In the checkout line at FedMart,
while Mother is waiting to pay, Susie
careens sideways and crumples. Fat faces
stare and I stare back until they look away.

Susie is unpredictable and often violent.
Plates and glasses are thrown. Squad cars
in the driveway are not uncommon.
Sedatives and syringes sleep in the fridge.
Mrs. Foster, the nurse who lives up the street,
comes to stick Susie when necessary.
Mother bakes a German chocolate cake for her
and dispatches me up Mott Street with it.

Rose Canyon slumps behind the house
with its ice plant, tumbleweeds and wild mustard.
While I'm in the backyard, playing horses,
there's a ruckus indoors.
Susie is howling something

that sounds like "kill me, kill me."
She is held down on the bed
by Mother, Daddy, Stephanie, Doug,
each with a limb.
This scene does not involve me.
I'm not even sure that I actually see it.

Doug scolds me when I laugh
during the earthquake but the dancing
bird bath looks funny to me, green
algae-laced water sloshing from its tipsy
Red Skelton mouth onto the ochre bricks
below. Where are the sparrows and their
old compadres the gullible house cats?
Doug drags me by the wrist
(he won't touch my hand). The house
remains upright, undamaged.
The house says, nothing happened here.

Stephanie and I play a game
of Susie. I pretend to be Susie.
I knock on the bedroom door and say,
"Stephanie, Mother says you have to come
and get into the … dog." I pretend that I can't
remember the word for car. This makes us roar.

1969, Mesa Vista Hospital for "acute psychosis."
Hydrocephalus. Pressure on the brain.

Susie is rolled in an old green army blanket
to immobilize her during one of her rages.
She is deposited on the Chevy wagon's
middle seat to be driven to the hospital.
Daddy stands in the garage beside the car
and he is weeping.

1972, a low-pressure ventriculoperitoneal
shunt to drain the fluid. An infection.
The shunt requires replacement later that year.

1973, a neurilemmoma. Craniotomy.
After that, she is mute. A "neurologic cripple."

Our van has a hydraulic lift. Mother ties
Susie into the wheelchair, loads her
and drives to Del Taco where Mother
has a floury quesadilla and coffee with cream
in a Styrofoam cup, which she drinks
in the parking lot next to the Subaru dealership.
The ridiculous sun is always shining.

Past history. Refer to old chart.

Permanent tracheostomy and gastrostomy.
Mother pumps formula into the stomach tube.

1976, Susie is hospitalized yet again
for "abdominal distention and regurgitation."

Mother pumps food into Susie
and then Susie vomits it.

Medications: Diamox, Dilantin, Mysoline, Potassium Chloride
and other medications as per her mother's attached list.
Family History: Noncontributory.
Review of Systems: Noncontributory.

Agonal. She is in pain.
For years and years, pain.

Strapped upright in the wheelchair,
parked in front of the living room's

console TV for *Wheel of Fortune,*
eyes lolling, she is in pain.

She has been cared for at home by her mother, with some
occasional assistance from night nurses. This admission was
prompted when she seemed to be "going downhill," according to
the mother. She has had temperature, been less responsive, and
has not urinated normally. In addition, she has been agitated
and combative.

Her inhuman utterances,
the mouth crooked, saliva stringing.
Urine in the sofa, in the wheelchair,
in the canopied princess bed in the bedroom
across the hall from my room
where I stay up late late to watch
Johnny Carson, Tom Snyder.

The suction machine thumps and squalls.
If the trach tube is not cleared, Susie will suffocate.
Imagine a metallic hole in your trachea.
Now, a thin plastic tube going in, sucking.
I only think about how noisy it is.

The patient is unable to aid in any self-care.

Mother sleeps with her. Twin beds.
Daddy sleeps in the den as he always has.

Mother naps in the afternoon, when she can.
I see her sitting on the bed's edge, as if
she has just woken up, her head hanging.

The house smells like piss and shit.
The floral sofa is particularly redolent.
Sometimes there's an ambulance

in the driveway, red lights strobing.

I never think about her being in pain.

Mother bends Susie's arms and legs twice
daily in the room with the mirrored closet doors.
Sometimes Susie makes noises.
I do not think of them as moans.
It's just Susie.

*The patient has always been in the same mental state, virtually
comatose, since I have been seeing her. However, the mother
continues to notice changes in the level of consciousness, noting
that sometimes for periods of weeks to months she will respond,
watch television, smile, and Mrs. McCartney notes that Susan
has actually said several short sentences. Nonetheless, none of
those have ever been witnessed by any of the medical profession
and there is some question as to whether the changes are
perceived to be greater by the mother than they are.*

Mother will not put Susie in a nursing home.
Mother says, "She would be dead in a day!"

No one ever talks about it,
what has happened to our family.

She has urinary tract infections,
pneumonia, low-grade fevers.
Eventually, an indwelling catheter.
I never think about her pain,
her real physical pain.

*For years I have regarded her as being in a persistent akinetic,
mute or vegetative state secondary to her multiple brain
tumors, shunt and general debility. . . . It would appear to this
examiner that the combination of nonreactive pupils and*

absent doll's eyes, unresponsiveness, and respiratory depression
can all be related to progressive central nervous system
deterioration because of the effects of the numerous central
nervous system insults to this poor girl.

This poor girl. No one in the family says that.

When I run away from home,
to the beach, and am returned
twenty-four hours later by the police,
Mother chooses to converse with me
about my tribulations while washing
Susie. Arms, legs, genitalia.
I stare into the closet's mirrored doors.
I can see Susie behind me, naked and inert.
I realize that Mother is making A Point,
but I will not bow down.

We are stubborn.

1961, the doctors say Susie will not last
another six months, but she does.

Is there any value in exploring this?
Whatever you deny grows stronger.

Go there. Stop avoiding it.
Stop pretending it didn't happen.

Her prostration, slack hair, flaccid arms.
Mother heaving that thin, collapsed body
onto a fresh Chux. The cyanotic limbs.

She was in pain. Imagine any one
of your children in pain. For years.

Diagnoses:

1. *Occlusion distal valve of ventriculoperitoneal shunt.*
2. *Normal pressure hydrocephalus, controlled.*
3. *Grand mal epilepsy, controlled.*
4. *Status postoperative posterior fossa brain tumor, neurilemmoma (1973).*
5. *Status postoperative left temporal glioma (1961).*
6. *Feeding gastrostomy tube in place (1973).*
7. *Permanent tracheostomy in place (1973).*
8. *Status postoperative laparotomy for bowel obstruction (4-3-76).*
9. *Status postoperative scalp debridement for wound dehiscence over shunt tube (4-8-76).*

Mother is a martyr, but she's not a hero.
She gets tired and bitter and morose.
When Daddy buys a motorboat (his business
is doing well) and names it the *Susie-Q*,
Mother sneers, "He would buy her anything.
He would put a pool in the yard if she wanted it."

I want a pool. I would love to have a pool.

It was Dr. DeBolt's feeling, with which I concur, that there has been progressive CNS deterioration from her already low-level function over the past several months and that it was not unlikely that this was a central fever. In any event, it seems clear that no further medical work-up is likely to be helpful. . . . There was a long discussion with both Mr. and Mrs. McCartney by myself as well as by Dr. DeBolt regarding heroic measures and it was felt that because of Susan's general condition, resuscitation should not be undertaken.

Susie dies on September 29, 1979.

Daddy is with her when it happens. After,
he waits at the hospital's front doors to tell Mother.
Mother says, "Thank God it's over."
And walks back to her car.

I am away at college, but Daddy phones me
with the news. My knees go weak.
I have to sit down. I'm thinking,
"Wow, that actually happens."
I thought it was just a cliché.

There is a funeral, but Mother does not attend.

I come home at Christmas,
the first Christmas after Susie's death.
I bring my laundry and Mother does it for me.
When the dryer is finished, she dumps
the clean clothes in Susie's wheelchair
and trudges it down the hallway
to the mirrored bedroom where she irons
and folds and irons and folds.

Anorexica

A rage at the heart of it.

I do not owe you anything.
I do not have to eat.

The asshole on the street says, "Smile.
You're prettier when you smile."

I say, "Fuck the hell right off."

No, that's wrong.

What I actually do is smile.

The skinny girl in the college cafeteria
grins as if she knows me.

The worm of nothingness at the heart
of being. Sartre's worm.
That is what I embrace.
Out of nothingness, being.
Out of not eating, power.

By shrinking, I become more.

The egg whites, not the yolks.
The vinegar, not the oil.

Ten salted peanuts counted into a white bowl.
Masticated slowly, such richness
and warmth, while I read the Victorians.
Thomas Hardy. George Eliot. *Middlemarch.*

Middlemarch. Middlemarch.

I am Fanny Price, saying,
No, no, no, I will not.

Hand in hand with rage goes horror.
The scale up by a pound or two.

You can always eat less.
It's something you can always do.

The scale dropping is like money.
The way wealth provides room to manoeuvre.

No white sugar. No white flour.
Nothing white. A white problem.
Not wanting to be seen.

Do not look at me.

Now,
look at me.

Hunger is no longer something
that visits on occasion
but a resident. A boon.

The cute, sunburned cashier at Save-On smiles at me
as I purchase my *Glamour* and *Cosmo*.

At home, in my purple-shag bedroom,
I study the women, envying
their slimness, the ease with which
they navigate the circumvention of the page.

It's not lust. I do not want them.
I want to be them. Flat. Sharp.
Clothes loose on my limbs.

It is lust.

The being of consciousness is consciousness of being.
All knowing is consciousness of knowing.

I will grow thinner. And thinner.
Inertia and its negation.

Being thin is the thinness of being.
All hunger is hunger for consciousness.

Mother sitting in the chintz chair
with her sad plate of dinner.
Instant mashed potatoes. Frozen peas.

Both Mother and Father are what we call overweight
and unhappy about that. I am congratulated on losing weight.
Meanwhile, Susie is dying.

I make myself thin. I make myself a cliché.
I grow so thin that my period stops.

If in this world of abundance
only what is in limited supply

has value, well, then, I will
make myself scarce.

I pretend to read *Gourmet* and *Bon Appétit*,
but I only care about the pictures.

I bake. Chocolate cream pie.
Cayenne-dusted corn cake.
I do not eat.

There are things you can eat without gaining weight.
Dill pickles. Bick's cocktail onions.
Massive bowls of iceberg sprinkled with cider vinegar.
All manner of sourness. My sustenance.

Consciousness is the annihilation of consciousness.
Consciousness holds nothingness inside itself.

A wedge of raw green cabbage is sweet
to me. Luxurious.

I don't trust it.

I check the calorie counts
of my herbal tea, just to make sure.

In order to be conscious of consciousness,
we have to step away from consciousness.
The gap is nothingness.

The orange grove next door has been abandoned.
The trees broken. Soon, there will be a mansion.
Pink stucco with more bathrooms
than bedrooms and no basement.

Under the houses, red dirt.
Stepping into nothingness.
A desire to be beyond desire.

Outside, in my yellow rococo sundress,
exhilaration, beyond illusion.
My god is a god with a cleaving sword.

What has comfort ever done for you?
You can learn nothing from that.

Is this really a Diet Coke?
It tastes too good.

I send it back.

Hunger is always an elsewhere. An escalation of elsewhere.

By starving, I put myself into question.
I become nothingness.

Surrounded by affluence, the roll of twenties
in Father's pocket, I am the embodiment
of penury.

What I am trying to say is that the money
means nothing to me. I reject it all, as I reject
food. I will live to regret this.

All I see is abundance.
Things, things, things. And all I want
is nothingness:

The foundation of myself is as a lack of myself.
In becoming less, I unearth myself. Dirt.

The conatus of anorexia is disinclination,
disenchantment.

The full moon confers on the crescent moon
its status as crescent.

I hear the coyotes chattering at night.
Occasionally, a jackrabbit's scream.

I am the crescent moon, waning.
Behind me, the shadow, a rotundity.

The anorexic does not want to be thin.
The anorexic wants to be whole.

I despise the superficiality of my parents.
I don't know any better.

I want to be authentic. To keen.
How does one do that? Pare away
the excess, the adipose.

We fool ourselves with food.
We fool ourselves into thinking that it will be okay.
I will not lie to myself.

Hunger as an organic phenomenon,
as a physiological need,
does not exist.

Rather, the being of hunger is a being in itself
of a state for which there must be a transcendent witness.

While I am hungry, I transcend.

If desire is a lack of being, I become.
I transcend lack.

But this is a lie.

Lack is the root of being.
What is lacking is ubiquitous.

If I eat, I will be bereft and broken.

No. If I eat, I will be like everyone else.

I feel so weighed down, at times.
So heavy in my skeletal limbs. I want
to give them up to the ever-present,
to sink into the sand in front of the pricey
palatial bungalows of La Jolla Shores
and become nothing but quietude.
Atoms leaking into the salt-and-peppery sea.

It's the old familiar empty feeling,
how, when I look in the mirror,
I can feel that I am outside myself,
uncontained. Inside is nothing.

I know that I should eat,
yet I will not. I will be
that contradiction.

Turkey breasts seared in a non-stick pan.
Cherry tomatoes sliced in half, a smidge of salt.

Desire is always a movement toward beauty,
unity, stepping across the gap.
But unity implies the gap.

Sartre says that desire, by itself, tends to perpetuate itself,
always creating another horizon of possibilities.

If I lost enough weight, I could eat whatever I want.

Repletion is death, the loss of possibility.
Schrödinger's maximum entropy.

It is not about being thin.
It is about never being thin.

Not being thin is the negation
at the heart of the anorexic's being.

What we lack is lack.
Therefore, we create lack.

The fallacy here is that a lack
of lack remains a lack.

Mother's despair, her right-wing pundits.
Father's fear of riots, unrest, the underclass
rising. Long guns in the closet.
Loaded.

It's an effort to change, but I become
stuck in the desire to become.

How to get out of that? Stop the desire to change.
Give up the effort to control and coerce.
But the effort to give that up is a measure of control.

The desire to step out of inner conflict arises
from inner conflict and causes inner conflict.

Hungry, I drive down 101 by the beach below Torrey Pines.
Porpoises fling themselves.
Hungry, I walk in front of the shops of the Carlsbad mall.
Fashion Valley. The University Towne Centre.

I buy new outfits at Contempo Casuals
with the money that Father gives me.

Size 0.

Pride is always self-hatred.

Tomorrow
will be better. I will be thinner.

Years from now, I will walk out of the marriage.
Give up the husband
because I love him too much.
There is no other way.

This is not vanity. This is not frivolity.
This is not fashion magazines.
You want us to be that shallow.

A Marine pilot ditches
his Hornet in the canyon, killing four people.
The Marine survives.

Inherent in it is the idea that suffering
will be rewarded, that everything
will be right in the end.

I still believe this.

Fear, fear, fear.
Whatever you fear
is what you become.

I will live through it.
Others will not.

Just be.
Eat cinnamon toast.
Reckless abandon.

Prayer

Whatever death is,
please let it be quiet.

Acknowledgements

Thanks to the Canada Council for generous assistance
without which this book would not have been written.

"Agonal and Preterminal" appeared in the June 2016 issue of
Numéro Cinq.

Villa Negativa is Sharon McCartney's seventh volume of poetry. Her previous books include *Metanoia* (2016, Biblioasis), *Hard Ass* (2013, Palimpsest), *For and Against* (2010, Goose Lane Editions), *The Love Song of Laura Ingalls Wilder* (2007, Nightwood Editions), *Karenin Sings the Blues* (2003, Goose Lane Editions) and *Under the Abdominal Wall* (1999, Anvil Press). Sharon's poems have been included in several editions of *The Best Canadian Poetry in English*. She has an MFA from the University of Iowa's Writers' Workshop and an LL.B. from the University of Victoria and currently lives in Victoria, British Columbia.